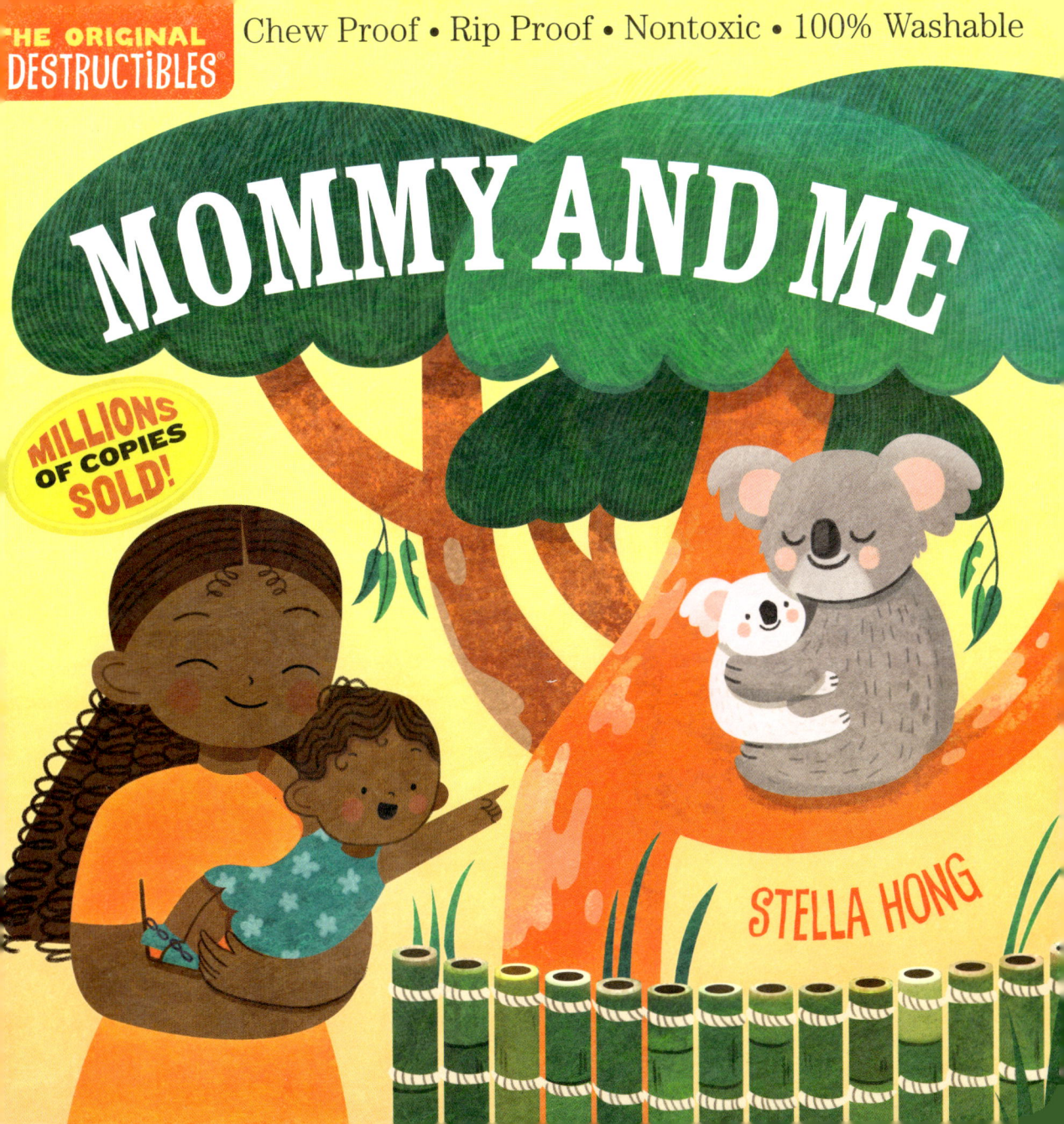

THE ORIGINAL DESTRUCTIBLES®

Chew Proof • Rip Proof • Nontoxic • 100% Washable

MOMMY AND ME

MILLIONS OF COPIES SOLD!

STELLA HONG

Mommy hugs baby

like elephant holds calf.

Mommy snuggles baby

as closely as puffin cuddles chick.

Mommy dances with babies

like deer frolics with fawns.

Mommy kisses baby

as sweetly as tiger nuzzles cub.

Mommies love their babies

12 301

more than anything
in the world.

For ages 0 and up!

Books babies can really sink their gums into!

We hug, just like elephant and calf!
We snuggle, just like puffin and chick!
We kiss, just like tiger and cub!

Celebrate the love between mommies and babies everywhere
in a book that's INDESTRUCTIBLE.

DEAR PARENTS: INDESTRUCTIBLES are built for the way babies "read": with their hands and mouths. INDESTRUCTIBLES won't rip or tear and are 100% washable. They're made for baby to hold, grab, chew, pull, and bend.

CHEW ALL THESE AND MORE!

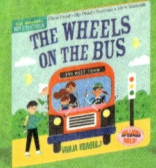 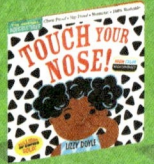 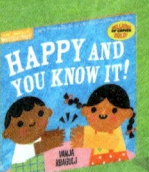 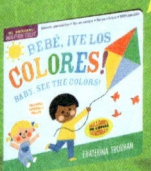 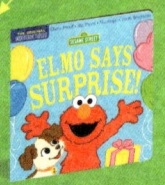

$5.99 US / $7.99 Can.
ISBN 978-1-5235-2875-2

50599

9 781523 528752

Distributed in the United Kingdom by
Hachette Book Group, UK, Carmelite House,
50 Victoria Embankment, London EC4Y 0DZ.
Distributed in Europe by Hachette Livre,
58 rue Jean Bleuzen, 92 178 Vanves Cedex,
France.
Contact special.markets@hbgusa.com regarding
special discounts for bulk purchases.

All INDESTRUCTIBLES books have been safety-
tested and meet or exceed ASTM-F963 and
CPSIA guidelines.
INDESTRUCTIBLES is a registered trademark of
Indestructibles, LLC.
Cover © 2025 Hachette Book Group, Inc.
First Edition March 2025 | 10 9 8 7 6 5 4 3 2 1
Printed in Shenzhen, China | IMFP

WORKMAN PUBLISHING • Hachette Book Group, Inc., 1290 Avenue of the Americas, New York, NY 10104 • indestructiblesinc.com